PARIS IN THE SIXTIES

PARIS IN THE SIXTIES

**EDITED BY
GEORGE PERRY**

PAVILION

Picture Editor: Suzanne Hodgart
Art Director: Grant Scott

First published in Great Britain in 2001 by
PAVILION BOOKS LIMITED
London House, Great Eastern Wharf
Parkgate Road, London SW11 4NQ
www.pavilionbooks.co.uk

A CIP catalogue record for this book is available from the British Library.

ISBN 1 86205 411 8

Colour reproduction by Bright Arts, Hong Kong
Printed and bound in Spain by Graficromo

10 9 8 7 6 5 4 3 2 1

This book can be ordered direct from the publisher. Please contact
the Marketing Department. But try your bookshop first.

Opposite: Trouble on the streets in 1968

n truth it was the best of times and it was the worst of times, except that Dickens had said that about another tumultuous era in the long history of Paris. Perhaps the 1960s were not quite as cataclysmic as the Terror, but the heady air of change carried with it much of the intoxication that must have swept across the densely crowded streets during the French Revolution.

A revolution of sorts had already happened with the collapse in tatters of the Fourth Republic in 1958, the event that brought the return of the great exile of Colombey-les-Deux Eglises. Charles de Gaulle, soldier, statesman and patriot, was perceived as the one man who could save France from the crippling economic consequences of years of colonial wars that had led to a succession of unstable governments rarely lasting more than six months in office. De Gaulle assumed the presidency in early 1959 as head of the new Fifth Republic, and his upright, imposing, beak-nosed presence loomed over the decade as an iconic symbol of France's grit, stubbornness and vulnerability. De Gaulle tended to make frequent appeals to the electorate, using television as the vehicle for his exhortatory declamations. His old-fashioned, formal bearing was at complete odds to the social changes that were sweeping the world and to which politicians such as the British prime minister Harold Wilson endeavoured to attach themselves.

Paris, with its characteristic self-confidence, brimmed with ideas and creativity. In the Post-War years writers such as Albert Camus and Jean-Paul Sartre had explored the premise of existentialism, the oneness of the individual in his or her own universe, an intellectual idea that had its origins in the 1930s but which was honed and developed by Parisian intellectuals and seems to have peaked in the 1960s. Sartre's partner was the formidable Simone de Beauvoir whose closely argued seminal work *The Second Sex*, published in 1949, was the driving force for much of the march of feminism in the 1960s. Her writings had a profound effect on a good deal of the literature of the time. The structuralist movement, with Claude Lévi-Strauss as its originator, became the primary influence in criticism and philosophy, its intention to simplify and isolate essentials, its effect to cloud the waters of discussion with an impenetrable murk of abstraction. Roland Barthes, another influential force, and a prime mover in the development of semiology, the analysis of signs in society, reinforced a Marxist spin to the argument. Paris, with its tradition of open-air sidewalk cafés favoured by the literati and their hangers-on, offered plenty of excuses to engage in on-going debate, much of it sadly sterile.

Where the force of artistic revolt was most apparent was in cinema. A group of young Parisian critics under the aegis of André Bazin had contributed to his periodical, *Cahiers du Cinéma*. Their central argument was pitched against what they regarded as 'the tradition of quality' that had led to an impersonal, literate, non-innovative style of film-making for which commercial French cinema was renowned. They demanded a freer camera technique, more use of locations, a relaxed style of acting and screenwriting, allowing themes to develop in a purely cinematic way. The gloss and polish of the well-made film could be abandoned in favour of a grainy, more immediate technique, with handheld cameras, imperfectly recorded sound, overlapping dialogue, abrupt editing and improvized dialogue.

For critics to become film-makers themselves is extremely unusual, but suddenly it happened on a major scale, and the New Wave was launched, with Jean-Luc Godard and François Truffaut in the vanguard, and a phalanx of others, among them Claude Chabrol, Eric Rohmer and Jacques Rivette, contributing. It was by no means a masculine monopoly. The writer Marguerite Duras was as much responsible for the impact of her screenplay of *Hiroshima Mon Amour* as the director Alain Resnais. In 1962 Agnes Varda made the influential *Cléo from 5 to 7,* and in the same year married Jacques Demy, whose sweet but hard-edged musical romance *Umbrellas of Cherbourg* won the main prize at Cannes in 1964. It was Truffaut and Godard who led the New Wave, the former achieving international success on a scale normally denied French film-makers with *Jules et Jim* in 1961, starring the iconic Jeanne Moreau at the centre of a triangle.

Even more celebrated as an international film icon in the 1960s was Brigitte Bardot, a former model who had been discovered by Roger Vadim and had appeared in a succession of lightly clad ingénue roles before making more serious films such as Godard's *Contempt*. Her blondeness, her pout and her voluptuous figure placed her on a par with Hollywood's most eminent sex symbol, Marilyn Monroe, who was found dead in her bed in 1962.

In that same year Paris lost Yves Klein, whose celebrity as an avant-garde artist and action painter had been forged by such masterworks as his Monotone Symphony in which a large ensembles of musicians played a sustained note for several minutes while naked girls covered with wet blue paint writhed on a canvas spread across the floor. Klein was a member of a group of painters known as the New Realists who tended to produce three-dimensional works such as dustbins filled with accumulated objects, layers of posters carefully torn to reveal interesting underlays, and assemblies of junk painted and displayed in provocative compositions. Although there was little cross-pollination, Paris was the world's leading art centre after New York.

Pop artists became celebrities almost as if they were pop stars. The decade was the first to elevate teenagers to a position in which they could influence tastes in music, and propel their idols to chart-topping acclaim. More mature audiences preferred Gilbert Bécaud, but the young were interested in Johnny Halliday, a Gallic counterpart in popularity to Elvis. The impact of The Beatles on Paris was lukewarm, and there were many empty seats for their debut appearances at the Olympia in early 1964, with Sylvie Vartan as a more powerful attraction. The aloofness towards them continued and in 1965, when they appeared at the Palais des Sports, *L'Express*, a news magazine founded in 1957, crowed that France almost alone of the countries of the Western hemisphere had refused to recognize their exceptionality.

The place of Paris as leader of the world of fashion has been sustained since the Second Empire, but the

1960s was the first decade in which the business was pitched directly at the young. Yves St Laurent took over the House of Dior on its founder's death in 1957. He was only twenty-one and quickly imposed his genius. But in 1962 he decided to tear up his contract. This led to a nervous breakdown and a lawsuit that he won, enabling him to establish his own firm, which unashamedly and with considerable brilliance targeted the youth market. His rival, André Courrèges, whose couture house was founded in 1961, astounded the fashion world with his 1964 collection, with much emphasis on loosely cut short skirts, stark bright colours and an ingenious use of new materials such as PVC. He was to claim that he invented the miniskirt, although the designer Mary Quant in London may well have got there first.

What then of the downside to the explosion of energy and innovation in the arts and popular culture? France's politics were dangerously unstable, even with the positively regal figure of de Gaulle at the helm. The war in Algeria which had led to an officers' coup to prevent a sellout of the settlers, and was to cost 12,000 lives, was the issue which had brought him to power. In 1961 the pro-independence movement FLN staged a demonstration in the heart of Paris. The police fired at the crowd. Officially three people were killed, but the reality was that hundreds of bodies were found floating in the Seine. Algeria achieved its independence and 700,000 angry colonials returned to France. De Gaulle narrowly escaped an assassination attempt in the Paris suburb of Petit-Clamart that had been staged by the OAS, the right-wing organization that fought to keep

Algeria under French colonial rule. It was but one of their terrorist activities, which included street killings, letterbox bombs and other explosive devices planted in public places such as cinemas.

Carnage on the streets was nothing new. Only eighteen years earlier in the tense days of the Liberation the armed resistance movement to the German occupation had emerged into the open to engage in bloody gun battles with isolated pockets of enemy forces. The long history of Paris has been violent and riotous, from when the Romans in 52 BC put to the torch the village of the Parisii fisherman on what is now the Ile de la Cité, the site on which they later built their own city of Lutetia. During the next two thousand years there were sackings, conflagrations, epidemics, massacres, revolutions, sieges, occupations and a succession of wars, none of which seemed to diminish Paris's greatness as a world centre of culture.

The greatest conflagration of the 1960s was yet to come. New architecture had burgeoned, with tower blocks for the working-classes in the outer districts replacing some of the shanty towns filled with immigrants. There was also a chain of satellite communities on greenfield sites outside the city (today mostly absorbed within the expanding conurbation), and new buildings in the inner city, the most controversial of which was the soaring and monumental Montparnasse office skyscraper on the Left Bank. In a move to decongest the centre of the city it was decided to demolish the huge market buildings of Les Halles and relocate at Rungis, south of the city. Meanwhile the Métro, Paris's antique underground railway system, underwent modernization with more lines and extensions, and new trains equipped with rubber-tyred wheels to lessen noise and increase acceleration. A regional express system was planned to enable commuters to travel from distant suburbs to their workplaces, often without the need for interchange.

As these developments progressed it seemed that the area which had not succumbed to the pace of change, but was still rooted in fustian tradition, was education. The numbers of students had increased but the facilities for them remained static so that lecture halls, laboratories, canteens and lodgings were crowded to the point of collapse. Bureaucracy insisted on arcane rules to be followed, while teaching staff remained indifferent to the growing tide of dissatisfaction.

The cauldron popped its lid in 1968. Around the world students had been engaged in revolt, but the rebellions in Paris made many of them look tame. The leader was a sociology student at Nanterre, Danny Cohn-Bendit, dubbed by the press 'Danny the Red' after he had led a successful sit-in which had given the authorities cause to consider deporting him to Germany, his country of origin. Following an attack on an American Express office a student was arrested. This was the starting point for unrest that became so serious the authorities decided to close down the Nanterre campus. The rioters shifted attention to the Sorbonne on the Left Bank, and huge numbers of students swarmed into the surrounding streets, uprooting items of street furniture to form makeshift barricades against the police, an unconscious echo of the same methods that were used during the Commune rising of 1871.

For days students bombarded their opponents with stone setts torn from the cobbled road surfaces and with Molotov cocktails. The police, reinforced by contingents from beyond Paris, retaliated with tear gas and brutal charges. The horrified nation watched events on television. The malaise spread across France, affecting industry and services, and the country was paralysed by widespread strikes. The Cannes Film Festival was abandoned following a dramatic declaration by the president of the jury, Jean-Luc Godard, who regarded it as impossible to continue while Paris was in uproar.

Eventually de Gaulle called for his supporters to rally, and over 100,000 marched along the Champs Elysées, effectively ending the rebellion. The next year, following a referendum that he lost, the General resigned, returning to Colombey-les-Deux Eglises, where he died in 1970.

So ended Paris's turbulent decade.

Previous page: Actress Brigitte Bardot on wheels in the Bois de Boulogne

Right: Brigitte Bardot in provocative mood on a film set

Above: Savouring the evening air at Le Drugstore

Left: Cruising the boulevards in a Cadillac

**Left: A quick look
at *L'Express***

**Right: Joan of Arc still
involved in protest**

Left: Catching the fallout, 1968

Below: The face of order in 1964

Overleaf: Students rip up the street in 1968

Juliet Greco on stage (left) and singer Edith Piaf in a studio (above)

Above: Cool sounds on the Rive Gauche

Right: Alberto Giacometti in his studio

Puffing directors – Jean-Luc Godard
and Claude Chabrol – confer

Above: Deneuve enjoys her fantasy in
Belle de Jour

Left: Serge Gainsbourg with a poster
of actress Catherine Deneuve

Jane Birkin and Serge
Gainsbourg in the
film *Slogan*

Right: Serge Gainsbourg and partner Jane Birkin rehearse

Below: Serge and Jane at work and play

Breaking the cordon in 1968

Left: Pierre Cardin welcomes actress Jeanne Moreau to his fashion show

Right: Architect Le Corbusier prepares to paint

Left: Yves Klein, action painter

Above: Klein prepares for body art

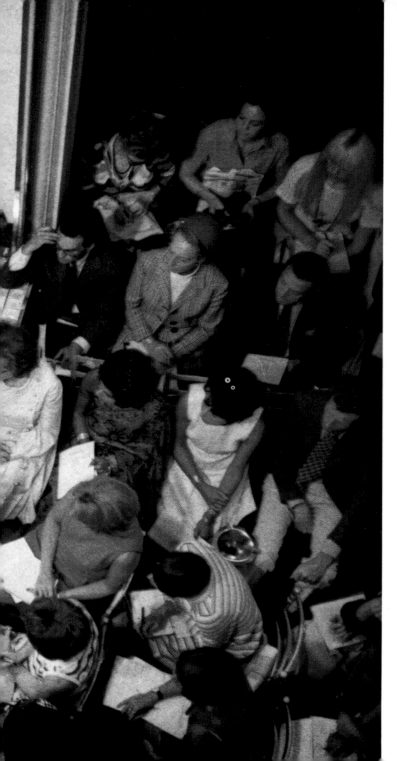

Above: Fashion designer Yves Saint Laurent

Left: YSL parades his models

Above: Director Jean-Luc Godard with
Brigitte Bardot and Michel Piccoli

Left: Françoise Sagan, novelist (centre)
with Yves Saint Laurent to the right

43

Left: François Truffaut, director and critic with his cardboard idol

Below: Movie sisters: Françoise Dorleac and Catherine Deneuve

Left: Enjoying a smoke with Che Guevara

Above: Danny Cohn-Bendit, revolutionary leader

Left: Students march along the Champs Elysées

Below: American Express is smashed

Union leader Benoit Franchon addresses
the Syndicat

Left: Zipped
jackets highlight
young fashion

Right: Style at the
flea market

Above: A student couple in their apartment at the start of May 1968

Left: Actors Mireille Darc and Jean Yanne in Godard's *Weekend*

Playwright Jean Genet enjoys a cigar at a café

**Above: Jean Paul Sartre, existentialist
and Simone de Beauvoir, feminist**

Left: Samuel Beckett, literary guru

Marguerite Duras, literary doyenne

Playwright Eugene Ionesco deep in thought

LA CHIENLIT C'EST LUI!

Left: President De Gaulle is the one who fouls the bed

Right: Hawking a left-wing paper on the streets

Left: Movie director Louis Malle, over the camera

Right: Alain Resnais, editing

Actor Jean Paul-Belmondo and actress
Ursula Andress attend his movie premiere

Above: The war of the posters

Left: Police turn nasty – 1968

Overleaf: Paris café life goes on

Left: André Courrèges,
fashion's new
eminence, 1965

Right: Yves St Laurent's
1966 models and
the transparent look

Above: Police take over the barricades

Right: The red flag is raised

1968: Protest in print (left), but some remain unimpressed (above)

Above: Film-maker Agnes Varda directs *Cléo from 5 to 7*

Right: Jean-Luc Godard directs *The Seven Deadly Sins*

Overleaf: A lone student takes on the law

Left: Entertainer Sacha
Distel twists with singer
Paul Anka

Right: Yves Saint Laurent
backstage with his models

**Left: Singer Gilbert Bécaud
in action**

**Right: Jean-Luc Godard's wife
and star, Anna Karina**

Singer Johnny Halliday snatches a bite (above) and pleases the fans (right)

Below: The flames of summer 1968

Right: Pavement artist and psychedelic imagery

Left: Café window scene

Below: Late night record store

Left: Twilight of Les Halles

Right: Street talk

Summer sunbathing 1968

Exposed butcher's shop in Les Halles

LA PLUS BELLE ÉVAS
DU SIÈCLE : Holin, l'éminence
de François Ca

**Left: Belmondo
puts on the style**

**Right: More style on
the Champs Elysées**

Brigitte Bardot and flashy table hoppers

**Left: Producer Raoul Lévy and Jeanne Moreau
at a film preview**

**Right: Actor Yves Montand and wife,
actress Simone Signoret, attend a premiere**

Supporters of the Vietcong

Left: Prêt-à-porter models pose in a café

Right: The summer of 1968

Charonne tragedy mourners at the funeral, 1962

Left: A hippie store opens

Right: A miniskirt rises

Singer Françoise Hardy takes the stage

Left: Director Alain Resnais
and his star,
Genevieve Bujold

Right: Actress Mireille Darc

De Gaulle's supporters
on the march

Left: Anger in the street

Overleaf: They shall not pass

PHOTO CAPTIONS

Page 17: The inflammatory Algerian conflict that conditioned French politics for much of the 1960s was frequently ventilated on Paris streets. Here two protestors use the statue of Joan of Arc as a prop for their crude sign.
Corbis Sygma

Page 18: An injured woman, an innocent victim of the street battles in 1968, is given sympathetic support as she seeks first aid.
Corbis Sygma

Page 19: President Charles de Gaulle arrives to an official greeting at the Hotel de Ville in 1964.
Raymond Depardon/Magnum

Pages 20–1: Student rioters combat police tear gas by hurling paving stones in the Rue St Jacques on the Left Bank during the unrest of May 1968.
Hulton Getty

Page 22: The singer Juliette Greco performing at the Bobino theatre.
Guy Le Querrec/Magnum

Page 23: Edith Piaf, the legendary singer, during a recording session at the Pathé Marconi studios in 1961.
Nicolas Tikhomiroff/Magnum

Page 24: The Club St Germain des Prés resounds to cool jazz as young Parisians dance the night away. Although in the 1960s the beat of the disco seemed all-conquering, on the left bank in Paris establishments such as this still managed to hold their own.
Camera Press

Page 25: Among a handful of 20th century artistic giants was the Swiss sculptor Alberto Giacometti, who studied in Paris in the 1920s and established his studio there. His constant experiments with form led to the characteristic matchstick figures for which he was universally recognized. He died in 1966.
René Burri/Magnum

Pages 26–7: The two smokers are Jean-Luc Godard on the left and Claude Chabrol, two notable film directors of the New Wave and writers for the monthly film magazine *Cahiers du Cinéma*.
Raymond Depardon/Magnum

Page 28: Serge Gainsbourg stands in front of a poster of actress Catherine Deneuve in 1968.
Odile Monteserrat/Corbis Sygma

Page 29: Catherine Deneuve enjoys a moment of fantasy in Luis Buñuel's black comedy *Belle de Jour*, made in Paris in 1967.
Corbis Sygma

Pages 30–1: English actress Jane Birkin and Serge Gainsbourg on the set of Pierre Grimblat's 1969 film *Slogan* in which they both appeared.
© Gilles Caron (Contact Press Images)

Page 32: Serge Gainsbourg and his partner Jane Birkin enjoy a joke and a smoke.
John Kelly/Camera Press

Page 33: Serge Gainsbourg and Jane Birkin rehearse, a month after their daughter Charlotte, now also an actress, was born.

The couple achieved international success with their record '*Je t'aime, moi non plus*' which, with its orgasmic sighs and heavy breathing, inflamed the censorious world over.
Giancarlo Botti/Camera Press

Pages 34–5: A rioter runs through a cordon in May 1968.
Marc Riboud/Magnum

Page 36: Fashion designer Pierre Cardin greets the actress Jeanne Moreau at his 1964 Collection.
Corbis Sygma

Page 37: Le Corbusier, architectural doyen, prepares to paint in his 16th Arrondisement studio, 1960.
René Burri/Magnum

Page 38: Yves Klein, influential, self-publicizing painter who died suddenly in 1962, aged 34.
© Pierre Boulat/Cosmos/Katz

Pages 38–9: Yves Klein supervises a paint-covered nude model about to create a 'body art painting' for him.
René Burri/Magnum

Page 40: A bird's-eye view of a Yves Saint Laurent fashion show in 1969.
© M.F./Rapho/Network

Page 41: Fashion designer Yves Saint-Laurent is flanked by his models Betty Calroux and Louise de la Falaise.
Hulton Getty

Page 42: Françoise Sagan, novelist with Yves St Laurent on the right.
© Pierre Boulat/Cosmos/Katz

Page 43: The director Jean-Luc Godard with Brigitte Bardot and Michel Piccoli, while directing *Le Mépris*.
© G. Dussart/Rapho/Network

Page 44: The film director François Truffaut in 1963 in front of a cinema showing Alfred Hitchcock's *The Birds*. A life-size cutout of Hitchcock, Truffaut's idol, is behind him. Truffaut's *Conversations with Hitchcock* was one of the most notable film books of the decade.
© Pierre Boulat/Cosmos/Katz

Page 45: Sisters and movie stars, Françoise Dorleac and Catherine Deneuve. Dorleac (the elder) died in a car crash in 1967 after they had appeared together in Jacques Demy's *Les Demoiselles de Rochefort*.
Corbis Sygma

Page 46: A 1968 student with a poster of Che Guevara in the background.
Rex Features

Page 47: Daniel Cohn-Bendit, the charismatic leader of the 1968 striking students, known as Danny the Red, addresses a rally at the Gare de l'Est.
Hulton Getty

Page 48: The Champs Elysées is filled with marching students as the tricolour flag of France is waved from the Arc de Triomphe.
Hulton Getty

Page 49: An attack on the American Express bureau by members of the Anti-Vietnam Committee in March 1968.
© Gerard Aime/Rapho/Network

Pages 50–1: Benoit Frachon, trade union leader, rallies his members as industrial unrest takes hold in May 1968.
Marc Riboud/Magnum

Page 52: Characteristic mid-1960s Paris fashions feature exaggerated zipped jackets for both sexes.
Rapho/Network

Page 53: Fashion at the Flea Market, another traditional Parisian institution.
Rex Features

Page 54: Actors Mireille Darc and Jean Yanne in Jean-Luc Godard's 1967 satire on the car-owning culture *Weekend*.
Corbis Sygma

Page 55: A young couple who are students at the University of Paris photographed in their apartment in the shadow of Ste Severine, on 1 May 68, the ominous month.
Jonathan Blair/Corbis

Pages 56–7: Jean Genet was a delinquent child who became an honoured literary eminence. Here he is photographed in the afternoon sun of a café terrace.
Henri Cartier-Bresson/Magnum

Page 58: Samuel Beckett, ex-patriate Irish-born writer, made his home in Paris from 1937 onwards and wrote extensively in French, becoming a fixture of the literary scene.
Jack Nisberg/Camera Press

Page 59: Jean Paul Sartre and Simone de Beauvoir, respectively gurus of existentialism and feminism, wielded considerable influence in intellectual circles in the 1960s.
Jack Nisberg/Camera Press

Pages 60–1: The writer Marguerite Duras, screenwriter of the Resnais film *Hiroshima Mon Amour*, enjoys a Gitane.
Bruno Barbey/Magnum

Pages 62–3: The playwright Eugene Ionesco in his office and work room in 1962.
© Marc Riboud/Magnum

Page 64: A 1968 student riposte to de Gaulle's notorious description of the rebels as 'ones who shit in the bed'. The slogan says: 'The bedshitter is him'.
Leon Herschtritt/Camera Press

Page 65: A street seller tries to peddle a left-wing paper to well-dressed pedestrians.
© Fred W. McDarrah

Page 66: Louis Malle (background) on the set of his 1966 film *Le Voleur*. The cinematographer was Henri Decäe.
Martine Franck/Magnum

Page 67: Alain Resnais, the director of the gnomic *Last Year in Marienbad*.
© Robert Doisneau/Rapho/Network

Pages 68–9: Actors Ursula Andress and Jean Paul-Belmondo at the premiere of the Louis Malle film *Le Voleur*. Belmondo played the lead.
Raymond Depardon/Magnum

Pages 70–1: During the early stages of the revolt led by left-wing student groups in May 1968, the police took on the rioters with force. This demonstrator is savagely clubbed in front of the stunned customers of a Wimpy bar.
Corbis Sygma

Page 71: The temperature of the time. Anti-Gaullist flyposters in 1968.
Martine Franck/Magnum

Page 72: A traditional aspect of Parisian street life, the coffee house with outdoor tables. This example, popular with artists and students, is on the Boulevard St Germain.
Paul Almasy/Camera Press

Page 73: Men read as they enjoy their drinks, apparently ignoring a girl sipping a drink on her own in the awning-covered heated terrace of a café.
Paul Almasy/Camera Press

Page 74: André Courrèges, the fashion designer who stole the acclaim at the 1965 Collections.
© Pierre Boulat/Cosmos/Katz

Page 75: Transparent dresses from Yves St Laurent's 1966 Collection.
© Pierre Boulat/Cosmos/Katz

Page 76: The aftermath of the May 1968 riots. The improvized barricades are inspected, as the magnitude of the clear-up task is assessed.
© Gilles Caron (Contact Press Images)

Page 77: The spirit of 1968 – a young woman raises the red flag at the rally of the National Union of French Students and Unified Socialist Party at the Charletty Stadium on 27 May.
Corbis Sygma

Page 78: A student holds up a left-wing newspaper during the riots of May 1968.
Rex Features

Page 79: Young street people photographed in July 1968.
© Fred W. McDarrah

Page 80: Agnes Varda, one of the most accomplished female film-makers, assesses a shot for her 1962 film *Cléo from 5 to 7*. Varda also wrote the screenplay.
Roger-Viollet/Frank Spooner Pictures

Page 81: Nicole Mirel and Eddie Constantine await the direction of Jean-Luc Godard (with sunglasses) for his section of the 1961 portmanteau film, *The Seven Deadly Sins*.
Roger-Viollet/Frank Spooner Pictures

Pages 82–3: The Rue St Jacques under attack in May 1968. A student has just hurled a projectile at the police who were regrouping after an earlier mêlée, which left the street littered with debris and lost shoes.
Corbis Sygma

Page 84: Entertainers relax: Sacha Distel, born in Paris in 1933, and the Canadian pop singer/songwriter Paul Anka try the twist at Régine's night club.
Frank Spooner Pictures/© Lipnitzki-Viollet

Page 85: Yves Saint Laurent with models at his couturier house as they prepare for a fashion show.
© Gilles Caron (Contact Press Images)

Page 86: The smooth singer Gilbert Bécaud performs before his rapt fans at the Olympia in 1962.
Frank Spooner Pictures/© Lipnitzki-Viollet

Page 87: The dark-haired actress Anna Karina, born in Copenhagen in 1940, became closely identified with New Wave cinema, mostly in the rush of exciting films that were made by her then husband Jean-Luc Godard, including *Une Femme est Une Femme, Vivre Sa Vie, Bande a Part, Alphaville, Le Petit Soldat* and here, *Pierrot le Fou.*
Corbis Sygma

Page 88: Johnny Halliday, singing idol of Parisian teenagers, grabs a bite at a 1961 appearance, early on in his career.
Corbis Sygma

Page 89: Johnny Halliday in performance in Musicorama 1966.
Nogues/R.A./Corbis Sygma

Page 90: Mayhem on the streets during the May 1968 disturbances. Police in riot gear watch as a vehicle blazes.
Bruno Barbey/Magnum

Page 91: A street artist adapts contemporary psychedelic style to his work.
© Fred W. McDarrah

Page 92: In the summer of 1968 a girl pauses over her coffee-time reading to eye the street.
© Fred W. McDarrah

Page 93: Round-the-clock shopping affects the Champs-Elysées, with browsers in a large music store exercising their newfound prosperity as they select albums.
© Erich Lessing/Magnum

Page 94: The twilight of Les Halles, the great central Paris market that was to be relocated in the outer district of Rungis.
Henri Cartier-Bresson/Magnum

Page 95: The itinerant young in the summer of 1968.
© Fred W. McDarrah

Page 97: The other face of summer 1968. Sunbathers make the most of available space at the Deligny pool alongside the Seine.
© Gilles Caron (Contact Press Images)

Pages 98–9: The old, unhygienic, congested market district of Les Halles shortly replaced by a palatial new site to the south of central Paris.
© Fred W. McDarrah

Page 100: Jean-Paul Belmondo, France's leading young movie star, as he appeared in Robert Entrico's *Ho!*
Raymond Depardon/Magnum

Page 101: This model crossing the Champs Elysées wears a silver kidskin minidress with matching belt, boots, hat and bag in the same material. The designer is Durer and the date is 1966.
UPI/Corbis

Pages 102–3: France's sex-kitten of the 1960s, the film star Brigitte Bardot, attracts the attention of table hoppers in a Parisian boîte.
Jack Nisberg/Camera Press

Page 104: The producer of *Moderato Cantabile*, Raoul Levy, with the star of the film, Jeanne Moreau, following a preview.
Roger-Viollet/Frank Spooner

Page 105: Yves Montand and his wife, actress Simone Signoret, surrounded by photographers at the Paris premiere of the film *Grand Prix*, in which he starred.
© Gilles Caron (Contact Press Images)

Pages 106–107: Pro-Vietcong demonstrators in the Avenue Kléber wave encouragement during the unproductive Paris peace talks in the late 1960s.
Leon Herschtritt/Camera Press

Page 108: Modelling 1964 prêt-à-porter fashions by Dior and Laroche in a café.
© Pierre Boulat/Cosmos/Katz

Page 109: Summer of 1968. Backpackers trudge along dusty boulevards.
© Fred W. McDarrah

Pages 110–11: Sombre faces mark the mourners at the funeral of victims of the 1962 Charonne tragedy. To escape a police charge, demonstrators in favour of Algerian independence ran to the Charonne Métro station but the gates were barred. In the crush several died from suffocation.
Henri Cartier-Bresson/Magnum

Page 112: The hippie look takes hold as a store opens on the Boulevard St Michel, close to the Sorbonne, in 1967.
Corbis/Bettmann/UPI

Page 113: A matronly woman eyes a miniskirt at the Brasserie Lipp.
Henri Cartier-Bresson/Magnum

Pages 114–15: Pop singer Françoise Hardy in performance.
Topham

Page 116: The actress Genevieve Bujold with the director Alain Resnais in a quiet, damp side street.
© Gilles Caron (Contact Press Images)

Page 117: The popular actress Mireille Darc who played a leading role in Jean-Luc Godard's remarkable 1967 satire *Weekend.*
Collection Viollet/Frank Spooner Pictures

Pages 118–19: In 1962 President De Gaulle, striving to end the Algerian crisis, dissolved the National Assembly in order to pursue his own constitutional referendum. Hundreds of thousands of supporters gathered to pledge support and marched up the Champs Elysées, led by Gaullist mayors.
Giancarlo Botti/Camera Press

Pages 120–1: The face of protest, 1968. A girl student unconsciously echoes the gestures of her ancestors of 1789.
Giancarlo Botti/Camera Press

Page 122–3: They Shall Not Pass. A line of police with drawn batons faces down the Champs Elysées with the Arc de Triomphe in the background.
Rex Features

Pages 128: 1968 Graffiti, 'the revolutionary theatre is in shit street'.
© Fred W. McDarrah